50 Science Questions for Curious Minds

By

Coby Tunnicliffe

First Edition 2023

Acknowledgments

The majority of these questions are not my own. The list of questions that became this book started at the back of a teacher planner where I would write down questions students asked me I did not know the answer to. I would tell students I would *look into it* and get back to. Therefore, I must say thank you to all the students who have asked me incredibly random questions that have led me down rabbit holes where I have often only found a half suitable answer and several more questions.

I also must acknowledge the contribution of AI in this work. Modern AI has helped me turn the rough notes of a science teacher into something that hopefully vaguely resembles professional pros.

Illustrations

All the illustrations in this book have been created with AI. The pictures are not scientifically accurate, DNA does not have a face and eyes for example! Instead, the aim of the images is to make certain sections more memorable and interesting. I also hope they give the reader an idea of the type of images that can be produced by AI in the 2023.

An Introduction

Welcome to an enlightening exploration of the wonders of science. This book is designed to guide you through a series of intriguing scientific inquiries, answering questions that often spark curiosity and wonder. Here, we delve into a range of topics, from the everyday phenomena we encounter, like the tears induced by an onion, to the grand workings of the cosmos that light up our night skies.

As you peruse these pages, you will find explanations articulated in a manner accessible to all, regardless of your prior knowledge of science. This book aims not just to inform but to ignite a deeper interest in the natural world and its many mysteries.

Each topic is addressed with the intent of shedding light on the how's and whys of nature, presented in a manner befitting both the casual reader and the keen learner of all ages.

The Questions

Why Does Cutting an Onion Make you Cry?

Chopping onions is a notorious trigger for tears, but the reason lies within a sophisticated chemical defence system of the onion. This begins at the microscopic level, where onions contain compartments that store amino acid sulfoxides. These compounds are relatively inert on their own, but when you cut into an onion, you break the cellular barriers, causing the sulfoxides to mix with enzymes. This sets off a series of chemical reactions.

The first reaction transforms the amino acid sulfoxides into a volatile, sulphur-containing compound, syn-propanethial-S-oxide. When released into the air and mixed with the water in your eyes, this compound forms sulfuric acid. Although very dilute, this acid is strong enough to stimulate the nerves in your eyes, causing a stinging sensation. The brain responds to this discomfort by signalling the lacrimal glands to produce tears, hoping to dilute and flush out the irritant.

The intensity of this tearful reaction can be influenced by several factors. The particular variety of onion, for example, can contain different levels of the enzyme and sulphur compounds, with some onions bred to be milder. A sharper knife will cause less cell damage, which means fewer of the tear-inducing chemicals are released. Moreover, cooler temperatures slow down the enzymes responsible for the chemical reactions, so refrigerating onions before cutting can reduce the amount of syn-propanethial-S-oxide produced.

To minimize tearing up, tactics such as chilling the onions, cutting under a vent or near a fan to disperse the gas, or wearing eye protection can be effective. Cutting onions under water is another method, as the offending chemicals are neutralized in the water rather than reaching your eyes. There's also the technique of leaving the root end intact while cutting, as it has a higher concentration of the compounds.

Through these adaptations and a bit of culinary strategy, we can outsmart the onion's natural defence mechanism and save ourselves a few tears in the kitchen.

Why do Apples Turn Brown After They're Cut?

When you slice into a crisp apple and leave it out, it soon loses its fresh appeal, turning an unpleasant brown. This browning reaction is a tale of exposure and oxidation, a common sequence of events in the chemistry of life.

At the forefront of this process are enzymes in apples called polyphenol oxidase (PPO). In an intact apple, PPO is sequestered in the cells, separate from phenols, which are also naturally present. However, when you cut an apple, you break open the cells. This rupture allows PPO to mingle with phenols, and oxygen from the air steps into this mix, facilitating a reaction that produces melanin, the same pigment that gives colour to human skin and hair.

This oxidative process is a defence mechanism for the apple, akin to how a cut on your skin scabs over. The melanin forms a barrier, albeit an unappetizing one for humans, that can help prevent the entry of pathogens. It's a swift reaction, often noticeable within minutes and more pronounced if the apple is at room temperature.

Temperature plays a crucial role in this chemical reaction. Cooler temperatures slow down the enzymatic activity, which is why refrigerated apples brown less quickly. Similarly, acidity can inhibit the enzymes, which is why applying lemon juice on a cut apple prevents browning. The acid adjusts the pH and acts as an antioxidant, adding a protective layer that fends off both oxidation and pathogens.

While the brown colour may not be visually appealing, it doesn't render the apple inedible. The browning does not significantly affect the nutritional value; however, it can slightly alter the flavour and texture, making it a less desirable snack.

Understanding the science behind an apple's browning can influence kitchen practices, such as chilling apples before slicing or using acidulated water to preserve their fresh, appetizing appearance for a salad or fruit platter.

Why Does Food Taste Different when its Cold?

Have you ever noticed that the leftover pizza from last night or the ice cream that melts on your tongue each offers a distinct taste experience when their temperatures change? This phenomenon is rooted deeply in the molecular dance between our taste receptors and the food we enjoy.

At warmer temperatures, the volatile compounds in food are more energetic, releasing more aroma and enhancing the flavour. Aroma plays a crucial role in our perception of taste, as much of what we consider "flavour" actually comes from smell. When food is heated, more aromatic compounds are released, which is why a hot meal can seem more flavourful. Moreover, our taste receptors are more sensitive when food is warm, allowing us to perceive the full range of flavours from sweet and salty to sour and bitter.

Conversely, when food is cold, the molecular activity slows down, diminishing the release of aromatics and thereby muting the flavour profile. The physical state of the food changes as well: fats solidify, altering texture and the way flavour compounds interact with our taste receptors. Cold can also numb the palate to a degree, making tastes seem less pronounced. This is partly why ice cream must be overly sweet when manufactured; as it cools, the perceived sweetness diminishes.

Additionally, temperature can affect the actual chemical structure of some flavour compounds. For example, cold can cause certain starches to retrograde, changing their texture and how they interact with other components of food, which can affect flavour. This is most noticeable in items like pasta or rice, which can taste different once they have been refrigerated and then reheated.

To understand the full depth of flavour, chefs and gourmands alike must consider temperature as a key ingredient. It's an aspect that can elevate the sensory experience of dining or be a critical factor in the appeal of foods designed to be consumed cold. So the next time you savour a dish, remember that its temperature is silently seasoning your experience.

How Does Soap Clean away Dirt and Oil?

Soap is a powerful tool for cleaning. It works well because it has two special parts. Imagine soap like a tiny magnet. One part of the soap loves water, and the other part loves grease and dirt. When you wash your hands with soap and water, the part of the soap that loves grease sticks to the oil and dirt on your hands.

The structure of soap molecules is akin to a pin, with a head that is attracted to water (hydrophilic) and a tail that repels water but readily binds with oils and fats (hydrophobic). When soap is lathered onto your hands with water, the hydrophobic tails of the soap molecules seek out and ensnare oils and bits of dirt. Meanwhile, the hydrophilic heads remain allied with the water.

As you continue to scrub, the soap molecules form spherical structures called micelles. Within these micelles, the hydrophobic tails are tucked safely inside, trapping the dirt and oil away from the water, while the hydrophilic heads face outward, ready to be rinsed away. This encapsulation securely sequesters the dirt, which is then swept away with the motion of rinsing, leaving surfaces clean.

Moreover, soap not only dislodges dirt physically but also assists in chemically breaking it down. This is especially effective against bacteria and viruses, which have lipid membranes. The soap molecules can wedge themselves into these membranes, prying them apart and rendering the pathogens harmless, hence the importance of handwashing in preventing the spread of disease.

Soap's cleansing action is greatly aided by mechanical action—rubbing or agitation—which enhances its ability to detach and lift away dirt. The combination of soap's molecular properties and the physical act of scrubbing enables the thorough removal of dirt, oil, and microbes, leading to a clean that is more than just skin-deep.

So, soap is like a helper that makes water stronger at cleaning. It's simple but very important for keeping our hands and bodies clean.

How Does Soap Kill Microbes?

Soap is remarkably effective at killing microbes, including bacteria and viruses. This effectiveness is due to the same structure that makes soap excellent for cleaning: its hydrophilic (water-loving) heads and hydrophobic (water-fearing) tails.

Many microbes, including viruses, are surrounded by a lipid (fat) layer. This layer, known as a lipid envelope, is crucial for the virus's ability to infect and replicate. When you wash with soap, the hydrophobic tails of the soap molecules are attracted to and insert themselves into this lipid envelope.

As you scrub, the physical action helps the soap molecules to surround and break apart this lipid envelope, much like how they capture grease and dirt. This action effectively dismantles the structure of the virus, rendering it inactive and unable to infect cells. For bacteria, soap works similarly by disrupting their cell membranes, causing the bacteria to break apart and die.

The process of forming micelles, as mentioned earlier, also plays a crucial role in removing microbes from the skin. As the soap breaks down the lipid envelopes or bacterial membranes, the remnants are encapsulated within the micelles. These are then rinsed away with water, removing the inactive microbes from your hands or any other cleaned surface.

Furthermore, soap's effectiveness against microbes is enhanced by the mechanical action of handwashing – the rubbing and friction help to physically dislodge and remove microbes from the skin. This is why thorough handwashing, not just a quick rinse, is necessary for effectively reducing microbial presence.

In summary, soap kills microbes by disrupting their lipid membranes, effectively dismantling their structure or rendering them inactive. Combined with the physical action of washing and rinsing, soap is a powerful tool against the spread of diseases, highlighting the importance of regular and thorough handwashing in maintaining health and hygiene.

Why Does Soap Taste Nasty?

Soap tastes nasty for a simple reason: it's made of chemicals that aren't meant for eating. Our taste buds are very good at detecting things that could be harmful to eat, and soap is one of those things.

The same special parts of soap that help clean our hands also cause the bad taste. Remember the soap magnet? One part loves water and one part loves grease. These parts are made of chemicals that taste very bitter to us. This bitter taste is a warning sign from our body saying, "This is not food, don't eat this!"

Long ago, our bodies learned to taste bitter things as bad because many poisons are bitter. So, the nasty taste of soap is actually a good thing because it stops us from eating something that could make us sick.

Why is Grass Green?

Grass, along with many other plants, is green because it has something called chlorophyll. Chlorophyll is very important for plants because it helps them use sunlight to make their food in a process called photosynthesis. The green colour we see comes from this special chlorophyll, which is really good at soaking up the sun's rays.

The sun gives off energy in the form of light. This light has many colours, like the ones we see in a rainbow. Chlorophyll loves the red and blue light the most, and it uses this light to turn water and carbon dioxide from the air into food for the plant. This food is a sugar, and it gives the plant energy to grow. Chlorophyll is not good at absorbing green light, though. Instead, it reflects this light. That's why our eyes see the grass as green.

All this happens in parts of the plant's cells called chloroplasts. These chloroplasts are like tiny factories inside the cells, where the food-making process happens. There are so many chloroplasts and so much chlorophyll in grass that it looks very green to us.

But why do plants have chlorophyll and not another colour? Well, it's because green light is not the strongest energy from the sun. By reflecting the green light and using the stronger red and blue light, the chlorophyll can make the most food for the plant.

Having lots of chlorophyll and being green also mean that plants can get enough light without getting too much. If they absorbed all the light, it could be too much energy, and that could hurt the plants.

So, grass is green because the chlorophyll in it is working to make food from sunlight, and green is the colour that is not used in this process. It's a sign that the plant is healthy and doing its job well.

Why Do Leaves Change Colour in the Autumn?

Leaves change colour in autumn because of changes in the amount of daylight and changes in the weather. During spring and summer, leaves serve as little food factories for the tree, thanks to a pigment called chlorophyll, which gives them their green colour.

Chlorophyll is crucial for photosynthesis, the process through which plants use sunlight to turn water and carbon dioxide into oxygen and glucose. This glucose is like a tree's food, giving it the energy it needs to grow. Chlorophyll is very good at using the sun's light, and while it's busy working, it makes the leaves look green.

But as the days get shorter and colder in autumn, trees prepare for winter. They start to shut down their food production. The chlorophyll breaks down, and the green colour fades. This reveals other pigments in the leaves that have been there all along, but they were just covered up by the strong green of the chlorophyll.

These pigments are carotenoids and anthocyanins. Carotenoids are responsible for the yellows and oranges in leaves, like the colours of corn, carrots, and bananas. They help with photosynthesis too, but they're not as good at it as chlorophyll and don't overpower its green colour until chlorophyll fades.

The variety of autumn colours we see—from yellows and oranges to reds and purples—is the result of the particular mix of these pigments in the leaves, which can be influenced by factors like the type of tree, the soil quality, and the weather.

Finally, as autumn progresses, the leaves are shed, helping trees to conserve water during the cold, dry winter months. This seasonal cycle of colour change not only creates a beautiful display but also serves an important purpose in the life of trees.

Why are There Different Seasons?

Different seasons happen because our planet Earth tilts on its axis as it goes around the sun. This tilt is not very big, but it's enough to affect the weather and cause seasons.

Imagine Earth like a spinning top, leaning slightly to one side as it moves in a big circle around the sun. Because of this lean, different parts of Earth get more or less sunlight at different times of the year.

When the Northern Hemisphere, the top half of Earth, tilts towards the sun, it gets more direct sunlight and warmer temperatures. This is when it's summer there. At the same time, the Southern Hemisphere, the bottom half, tilts away from the sun, getting less direct sunlight and cooler temperatures, which means it's winter there.

Half a year later, the situation is reversed. The Southern Hemisphere tilts towards the sun and enjoys summer, while the Northern Hemisphere tilts away, bringing winter. The spring and autumn seasons happen in the times between, when neither hemisphere is tilted strongly towards or away from the sun.

The closer you are to the equator, which is the middle line of Earth, the less you will notice these changes. The weather stays quite similar all year. But the further you go towards the poles, the North Pole or the South Pole, the bigger the changes in the seasons.

This tilt and the journey around the sun make sure that most places on Earth have four different seasons: spring, summer, autumn, and winter. Each season brings changes in weather, the amount of daylight, and in nature, such as different plants growing or animals behaving differently.

What is DNA and How Does it Determine our Traits?

DNA, which stands for deoxyribonucleic acid, is like a blueprint for living things. Every creature, from the tiniest bacteria to humans, has DNA. It's found inside the cells of our bodies, in a special place called the nucleus. DNA looks like a long, twisted ladder, or what scientists call a double helix.

The rungs of this ladder are made up of tiny bits called nucleotides, and the order of these nucleotides is really important. They are like letters in a book. They tell the cell how to build an organism, just like letters form words and sentences to tell a story. The order of the nucleotides in DNA forms genes, which are instructions for how the body should put together the things it needs to work properly.

These genes are why we might look like our parents. They decide things like what colour our eyes are, how tall we get, and even parts of our personality. It's like getting a mix of chapters from your mom's and dad's own life stories. This mix makes you unique, unless you have an identical twin, who has the exact same DNA as you.

However, DNA doesn't just decide how we look. It also can affect our health. Some diseases are caused by changes in the DNA sequence, which are like typos in the instructions. These changes can mean that parts of our bodies don't work as they should.

Even though DNA has all these instructions, that doesn't mean our life is completely decided by it. Our environment, like the food we eat, the air we breathe, and our experiences, can also influence how these genes work. So, while DNA gives us the basic outline for who we are, our lifestyles fill in the details of the picture.

Why do We Get Sunburned and How Does Sunscreen Work?

We get sunburned because of the sun's ultraviolet (UV) light. Our skin uses sunlight to make vitamin D, which is important for healthy bones, but too much sun can be harmful. There are two main types of UV light that can reach us: UVA and UVB. UVB is the one mainly responsible for sunburns.

The outer part of our skin has cells that contain a pigment called melanin. Melanin is like the skin's natural sunscreen. It helps protect our skin by absorbing UV light and stopping it from going deep into the skin where it can damage cells. When we're in the sun, our skin makes more melanin to try to protect us, and that's what makes us tan.

However, if we're out in the sun for too long, the melanin can't absorb all the UV light, and the excess UV can start to harm the cells in our skin. This can cause inflammation and turn the skin red, which is a sunburn. If our skin gets burned a lot over time, it can lead to more serious problems, like skin cancer.

Sunscreen helps protect our skin from UV light. It has special chemicals that absorb, reflect, or scatter the light, much like melanin, but it does this all over the body wherever we apply it. There are many types of sunscreen, and they come with different Sun Protection Factor (SPF) numbers. The SPF tells you how much UVB light the sunscreen can filter out. The higher the number, the more protection it offers.

Using sunscreen can prevent sunburn by creating a barrier that reduces the amount of UV light reaching the skin. It's important to use it properly: apply it generously all over exposed skin, and reapply it every two hours, or more often if swimming or sweating. Remember to also wear protective clothing, like hats and sunglasses, and try to stay in the shade when the sun's rays are strongest, usually from late morning to early afternoon. This way, you can enjoy the sun safely!

Why Can't Humans Breathe Underwater?

As hopefully you are aware, humans can't breathe underwater. This is primarily due to the stark difference in oxygen concentration between air and water. While air contains about 21% oxygen, well suited for our lungs to extract and supply to our bloodstream, water has significantly less available oxygen. This quantity can vary greatly, influenced by factors such as water temperature and whether the water is moving or still.

Colder water, for instance, can hold more dissolved oxygen than warmer water. This is because cold water molecules are closer together, which makes it easier for oxygen molecules to squeeze in between and stay there. That's why cold, mountain streams might have higher oxygen levels compared to warm, stagnant ponds.

Moving water, like rivers and streams, also typically contains more dissolved oxygen than still water. This is because as water moves, it mixes with air, and this agitation allows more oxygen from the air to dissolve into the water. In contrast, stagnant or still water has less opportunity to mix with air, which can lead to lower oxygen levels.

Despite these variations, even in the best conditions, the amount of dissolved oxygen in water is much lower than what is found in air. Our lungs are not adapted to extract the small amounts of oxygen from water. They are structured to handle air, which is less dense and richer in oxygen. The process of breathing involves the inhalation of air and the efficient extraction of oxygen by the lungs, something that cannot be replicated in a water environment due to the significantly lower oxygen content and the physical properties of water.

This fundamental difference in oxygen availability and our respiratory system's adaptation to air breathing means that humans require artificial means, like scuba gear, to breathe underwater. The design of such equipment considers the need to provide sufficient oxygen that our lungs can process, something natural water environments cannot offer us.

Can you Milk a Dolphin?

Female dolphins do produce milk, but it would be very difficult to milk one. This unique aspect of dolphin biology ties into their classification as mammals and the specialized adaptations they have developed for their aquatic lifestyle.

Dolphins are part of the mammalian order Cetacea, which also includes whales and porpoises. One of the defining characteristics of mammals is the ability to produce milk to nourish their young. In dolphins, as in all mammals, this is made possible by the presence of mammary glands. The milk from these glands is rich in fats and nutrients, crucial for the growth and development of the new-born calf.

However, the process of nursing in dolphins is significantly different from that in terrestrial mammals. In dolphins, the mammary glands are concealed within slits on the mother's abdomen. This adaptation allows the dolphin calf to nurse underwater while swimming alongside its mother. The calf feeds by latching onto the nipple, which is tucked away and not readily accessible like in cows or goats.

The practicality of "milking" a dolphin, therefore, is highly impractical and fundamentally different from milking terrestrial livestock. It's not just the physical differences in anatomy that make it challenging but also the natural behaviour and environment of the dolphins. They are highly mobile, aquatic creatures, and their nursing process is a part of their adaptation to life in the water.

How Does a Caterpillar Turn into a Butterfly?

This process of metamorphism, which takes place through several stages, is not only a change in appearance but a reorganization of the organism's body and lifestyle.

Egg Stage: The journey begins when a female butterfly lays eggs, often on a plant leaf. These eggs are small and can easily be overlooked.

Caterpillar Stage (Larva): In a few days, the eggs hatch into caterpillars. The primary task of these caterpillars is simple yet vital: eat and grow. Starting with their eggshell and then the plant they were born on, caterpillars consume voraciously, shedding their skin multiple times as they rapidly increase in size.

Pupa Stage (Chrysalis): When the caterpillar reaches a certain size and stage, it enters the pupa phase. Here, it forms a chrysalis around itself. Within this protective case, an extraordinary transformation occurs. The caterpillar's body undergoes a process akin to being rebuilt from scratch. Stem cells become active during this stage. These cells, previously dormant, utilize the nutrients stored from the caterpillar's earlier feeding phase to develop the various parts of the emerging butterfly.

Butterfly Stage (Adult): After some time, which varies among species, the adult butterfly emerges from the chrysalis. Its wings initially are wet and crumpled, but the butterfly soon pumps fluids into them, expanding them for flight. Once the wings are dry and fully extended, the butterfly is ready to take flight, beginning a new chapter of life.

In the butterfly's life cycle, we see a complete overhaul of the organism's structure and function, from the way it moves (crawling to flying) to its diet (leaves to nectar) and reproductive goals. The role of the caterpillar's stem-cell-like cells in this process is a testament to the transformative potential inherent in life, mirroring the capabilities seen in human stem cells used in medicine and research.

Why Does Hair Turn Grey as we Age?

The greying of hair as we age is a natural process and an intriguing aspect of human biology. It's not just a sign of getting older; it involves specific changes at the cellular level in our hair follicles.

Hair gets its colour from a pigment called melanin, which is produced by cells known as melanocytes. These melanocytes are located in the hair follicles, which are tiny sacs in the skin that hair grows from. When we're young, these melanocytes are quite active, continually producing melanin and giving our hair its colour, whether black, brown, blonde, or red.

As we age, however, the melanocytes gradually become less active and eventually stop producing melanin. Without melanin, new hair that grows in has no pigment, which makes it appear grey, silver, or white. The rate at which this happens varies greatly from person to person and is influenced by genetic factors.

But why do melanocytes stop producing melanin? Scientists believe it's linked to the aging of our cells and possibly to the accumulation of damage in our DNA over time. This damage can be influenced by various factors, including environmental factors like UV radiation from the sun and lifestyle choices like diet and smoking.

Interestingly, going grey isn't just about genetics or natural aging. In some cases, certain health issues, nutritional deficiencies, or stress can also cause premature greying. However, these instances are less common compared to the natural aging process.

Understanding why hair turns grey as we age also has broader implications in the field of biology, particularly in understanding how cells age and how aging affects cell function. While greying hair is a natural part of aging for most people, it also serves as a small window into the complex process of how our bodies change over time.

Why Do We Dream?

Dreaming, a universal human experience, occurs predominantly during a phase of sleep known as REM (Rapid Eye Movement) sleep, though it can happen at other sleep stages too. To understand why we dream, it's helpful first to understand what sleep is and its different stages.

Sleep is a complex biological process that's essential for our health and well-being. It's typically divided into two main types: REM sleep and non-REM sleep, the latter of which has three distinct stages.

Non-REM Stage 1: This is the lightest stage of sleep, often considered the transition phase between wakefulness and sleep. It's characterized by slow eye movement and reduced muscle activity.

Non-REM Stage 2: In this stage, eye movements stop, heart rate slows, and body temperature decreases. This period serves as a preparation for deep sleep.

Non-REM Stage 3: This is deep sleep, essential for feeling refreshed in the morning. During this stage, the body repairs tissues, builds bone and muscle, and strengthens the immune system.

REM Sleep: After about 90 minutes of non-REM sleep, REM sleep begins. This stage is characterized by rapid eye movements, increased brain activity, faster breathing, and temporary muscle paralysis. It's during REM sleep that most dreaming occurs.

Dreams are a series of thoughts, images, and sensations occurring in the mind during sleep. The exact purpose of dreaming is still a topic of research and debate. Some theories suggest that dreams help in processing emotions and consolidating memories. Others propose that they are a by-product of brain activity during sleep.

During REM sleep, the brain is active, and studies show increased brain activity in areas involved in processing emotions and memories. This activity might be the brain's way of processing and making sense of the vast amount of information we encounter daily.

In summary, dreaming mainly occurs during REM sleep, a phase marked by increased brain activity. While the exact reasons we dream are still not fully understood, it's believed to be related to processes involving memory consolidation and emotional regulation. Understanding sleep and its stages is crucial in appreciating the complex nature of dreaming and its role in our overall mental health.

Why Do We Get Hiccups?

Hiccups are caused by involuntary contractions of the diaphragm, the muscle at the base of the lungs that plays an essential role in breathing.

When you breathe in, your diaphragm pulls down to help pull air into the lungs. When you breathe out, it relaxes and air flows out of the lungs. A hiccup occurs when the diaphragm suddenly contracts instead of moving smoothly as it usually does. This sudden contraction causes you to breathe in air quickly, and the air rushing in hits your vocal cords, causing them to close suddenly. This closure is what creates the familiar "hiccup" sound.

There are many possible triggers for this sudden contraction of the diaphragm. Common triggers include eating too quickly, consuming hot or spicy foods, drinking carbonated beverages or too much alcohol, sudden changes in stomach temperature like drinking a hot beverage followed by a cold one, or even stress and excitement.

In most cases, hiccups last only a few minutes and are more of a nuisance than anything else. They're a natural reflex that everyone experiences, similar to sneezing or blinking. However, sometimes hiccups can persist for longer periods, which might indicate an underlying medical condition. Persistent or chronic hiccups, lasting more than 48 hours, can be caused by a variety of factors, including certain medications, medical conditions affecting the nerves or diaphragm, and gastrointestinal conditions.

The exact reason why we hiccup is still somewhat of a mystery to scientists. Some theories suggest that hiccups are a vestigial reflex, meaning they once had a purpose but are no longer necessary. For example, some believe they might have been useful for our ancestors or in foetuses and newborns for certain developmental reasons.

In summary, hiccups are caused by involuntary spasms of the diaphragm, triggered by various factors. While often harmless and short-lived, they are an interesting example of the many reflexes and involuntary actions our bodies can perform.

Why Do Some Medications Need to be Taken with Food?

Certain medications need to be taken with food for a variety of reasons related to how your body absorbs and reacts to these drugs. This guidance isn't just a casual suggestion; it can significantly impact the effectiveness of the medication and how well your body tolerates it.

1. **Enhancing Absorption:** Some medications are absorbed better when there's food in your stomach. Eating food activates your digestive system, and this can help your body to process and take up the medication more effectively. For example, some drugs are fat-soluble, meaning they dissolve and are absorbed better in the presence of dietary fat. Taking these medications with a meal, especially one that contains a little fat, can increase their absorption and make them more effective.

2. **Reducing Stomach Irritation:** Many medications can irritate the lining of your stomach. This is especially true for drugs like nonsteroidal anti-inflammatory drugs (NSAIDs), which can cause stomach pain, indigestion, or even ulcers if taken on an

empty stomach. Food can act as a buffer, protecting your stomach lining from direct exposure to these irritants.

3. **Controlling Side Effects:** Some medications can cause nausea or other gastrointestinal side effects. Taking them with food can help to mitigate these effects, as the food can help to settle your stomach and slow down the rate at which your body absorbs the medication, reducing the intensity of side effects.

4. **Maintaining Blood Sugar Levels:** Certain medications, particularly those for diabetes, can affect your blood sugar levels. Taking these drugs with food helps to balance their effect on your blood sugar, preventing spikes or dips that could be problematic.

It's important to follow your doctor's or pharmacist's instructions about taking medication with food. In some cases, taking medication on an empty stomach is necessary for its effectiveness, but in others, a meal can aid in absorption, reduce side effects, and protect your digestive system. If you're ever unsure about how to take your medication, it's best to consult with a healthcare professional for advice.

How Do Bees Make Honey?

Bees making honey is a fascinating and intricate process, showcasing nature's efficiency and teamwork. The journey from flower to honeycomb involves multiple steps and the collective effort of many bees.

1. Collecting Nectar: It starts with forager bees leaving the hive to collect nectar from flowers. Nectar is a sweet liquid produced by flowers to attract pollinators like bees. These forager bees use their long, tube-like tongues called proboscises to suck up the nectar and store it in their "honey stomachs" – a special part of their gut that holds the nectar separately from their food stomach.

2. Returning to the Hive: Once a forager bee's honey stomach is full, it returns to the hive. This is where the process of turning nectar into honey begins.

3. Passing the Nectar: Inside the hive, the forager bee transfers the nectar to worker bees by regurgitating it into their mouths. This might sound a bit gross, but it's an essential step in honey production. These worker bees chew the nectar for about 30 minutes. During this time, enzymes break down complex sugars in the nectar into simpler sugars, which makes the honey more digestible for the bees and less prone to bacterial growth.

4. Evaporation: Next, the bees deposit the processed nectar into the honeycomb. Here, water needs to be removed to turn it into thick syrup. Bees help this process by fanning the nectar with their wings, which increases air flow and helps evaporate the water from the nectar.

5. Capping the Honeycomb: When the honey is ready, it's much thicker than the original nectar. The bees then seal the top of the honeycomb with a wax cap. This sealing protects the honey and keeps it clean.

6. Using the Honey: Bees use honey as a food source, especially during winter. They produce much more than they need, which is why beekeepers can harvest the excess. When beekeepers extract honey, they make sure to leave enough for the bees to sustain themselves.

In summary, bees produce honey by collecting nectar, breaking it down into simpler sugars, and then evaporating the excess water. This process not only provides food for the bees but also results in the sweet honey that humans enjoy.

Is it a Bad Idea to Eat Grass?

Eating grass might seem like a harmless idea, but for humans, it's not the best choice. The main reason is that our digestive systems are not equipped to break down grass effectively. While grass isn't toxic, we simply can't digest it properly, which can lead to discomfort and nutritional issues.

Grass is primarily made up of cellulose, a complex carbohydrate that forms the structural part of plant cell walls. Cellulose is tough and resistant to digestion. In humans, the enzymes necessary to break down cellulose are lacking. This means that when we eat grass, we can't access the nutrients within it, and our bodies struggle to process it. Attempting to eat large amounts of grass can lead to stomach pain and other digestive issues due to this indigestibility.

In contrast, many animals, especially grazing ones like cows, sheep, and goats, have specialized digestive systems that can break down cellulose and extract nutrients from grass. Cows, for instance, are ruminants, which means they have a unique stomach with four compartments: the rumen, reticulum, omasum, and abomasum.

The rumen plays a crucial role in digesting cellulose. It's filled with billions of microorganisms, including bacteria, protozoa, and fungi, which break down cellulose through a process called fermentation. After initial digestion in the rumen, cows regurgitate a small amount of partially digested food, known as cud, and chew it again to further break it down, making it easier for the microorganisms in the rumen to do their job.

This complex system allows cows and other ruminants to derive nutrition from grasses and other fibrous plants, which are a major part of their diet. Humans, however, do not have this specialized digestive system. Our stomachs and intestines are designed to process foods that are much less fibrous than grass.

So, while eating a small amount of grass is unlikely to harm you, it's not beneficial either. Our bodies simply aren't designed to digest grass effectively, unlike the specialized systems in grazing animals like cows.

Are Chicken Nuggets Made of Dinosaurs?

Chicken nuggets aren't made of dinosaurs as we traditionally envision them, like T-Rex or Velociraptors. However, this quirky question touches on an intriguing scientific fact: birds, including chickens, are the modern descendants of a group of dinosaurs known as theropods. This evolutionary link is a fascinating part of our planet's natural history.

Theropods were bipedal dinosaurs, and evidence suggests that modern birds evolved from them. This connection is drawn from various similarities in bone structures and physical features observed in fossils. Fossils, the preserved remains of ancient organisms, offer crucial insights into this evolutionary path. Most fossils are formed from bones or other hard parts of organisms, which, over millions of years, become embedded in sediment and gradually turn into rock.

One significant challenge in studying dinosaur lineage is that DNA testing, a tool widely used to understand evolutionary relationships in living creatures, is not feasible with dinosaurs. DNA degrades over time and isn't preserved in fossils, which means we cannot directly analyse dinosaur

DNA. Our understanding of the link between dinosaurs and birds comes from comparative anatomy, the study of similarities and differences in the body structures of different species, and from analysing the fossil record.

Thus, while chickens are descendants of theropods, the birds we see today have undergone extensive evolutionary changes over millions of years. When we eat chicken nuggets, we're not eating the dinosaurs we know from museums and science books, but rather a very distant relative. This connection underscores the dynamic and ever-changing tree of life, demonstrating how species can evolve dramatically over time.

Why Does Salt Make Ice Melt?

Salt has the remarkable ability to make ice melt, and this phenomenon is closely related to the nature of solids, liquids, and gases, which are the three main states of matter. Understanding how salt interacts with ice involves a bit of chemistry and physics, particularly the concepts of freezing point and states of matter.

In solids, like ice, the molecules are tightly packed in a fixed structure and have limited movement. In liquids, such as water, the molecules are less tightly packed and can move around, allowing the liquid to flow. Gases, like water vapor, have molecules that are much further apart and move freely.

Water, in its solid state (ice), has a specific freezing point, which is 0 degrees Celsius (32 degrees Fahrenheit). This is the temperature at which it transitions between solid and liquid states. When salt is added to ice, it causes a disruption in the structured arrangement of water molecules in the solid state, leading to a lowering of the freezing point, a process known as freezing point depression.

The salt dissolves into the thin layer of water on the surface of the ice. It separates into its constituent ions, which then interfere with the formation of the ice structure. This interference prevents the water molecules from easily reforming into solid ice, even at temperatures below water's normal freezing point.

As a result of this, the ice begins to melt, turning into liquid water at a lower temperature than it would without the presence of salt. This is why salt is commonly used to melt ice on roads and sidewalks in cold weather, as it effectively lowers the freezing point of water, facilitating the melting of ice even in sub-zero temperatures.

Thus, the action of salt on ice is not just a simple reaction, but rather a fascinating interplay of chemistry and the fundamental properties of matter in its different states.

Why Does Sugar Dissolve Faster in Hot Water than Cold Water?

The reason sugar dissolves faster in hot water compared to cold water involves the principles of solubility, temperature, and molecular interaction. To understand this, let's first consider what happens when sugar is dissolved in water.

When sugar is added to water, the sugar molecules are attracted to the water molecules. In a process known as solvation, water molecules surround the sugar molecules and, through their interaction, pull the sugar particles away from the solid structure and into the solution. This process continues until the sugar is completely dissolved.

Temperature plays a crucial role in how quickly this process occurs. In hot water, the water molecules are moving much faster than in cold water. The increased movement means that the water molecules collide with the sugar molecules more frequently and with greater energy in hot water. These more frequent and more energetic collisions cause the sugar molecules to be dispersed throughout the water more quickly, speeding up the dissolution process.

Additionally, higher temperatures also increase the kinetic energy of the sugar molecules themselves, making them more likely to break away from the solid structure and interact with the water molecules. Essentially, the increased energy in the system – both of the water and the sugar – facilitates the breaking of bonds within the sugar and the formation of new interactions between the sugar and water molecules.

Another factor is that hot water can hold more dissolved sugar than cold water. This means there's a higher capacity for the sugar to dissolve before the solution becomes saturated.

Understanding why sugar dissolves faster in hot water than in cold water is an example of how temperature affects chemical processes and reaction rates. It's a principle that is widely applicable in cooking, chemistry, and various industrial processes, illustrating the intricate relationship between temperature and the behaviour of molecules in solution.

Why Does Milk Last Longer if you keep it in the Fridge?

The reason milk lasts longer when kept in the fridge is closely related to how temperature affects enzyme activity and the rate of microbial growth. Both of these factors play a significant role in the spoilage of milk.

Milk is a nutritious liquid, and like many other food products, it's susceptible to spoilage by the action of bacteria and enzymes. Bacteria are microorganisms that can thrive in milk, feeding on its nutrients and multiplying. As they do so, they produce acids and other waste products, which eventually cause the milk to sour and spoil.

Enzymes, which are proteins that act as catalysts for biochemical reactions, are also present in milk. These enzymes can promote various chemical reactions, including those that lead to spoilage. For instance, they can help break down fats and proteins in the milk, leading to changes in flavour, smell, and texture.

The rate at which both bacteria grow and enzyme's function is heavily influenced by temperature. Most bacteria and enzymes involved in milk spoilage thrive at warmer temperatures (around room temperature). However, when milk is stored in a fridge, the cold temperature significantly slows down their activity.

At lower temperatures, the enzymes in milk become less active. This means that the chemical reactions they catalyse, including those that lead to spoilage, occur more slowly. Similarly, the growth rate of spoilage-causing bacteria is greatly reduced in the cold environment of a fridge.

By slowing down the activity of enzymes and the growth of bacteria, refrigeration extends the shelf life of milk. It's a simple yet effective way of preserving the freshness and quality of milk by controlling the temperature to inhibit biological activity that would otherwise lead to spoilage.

In summary, keeping milk in the fridge prolongs its shelf life by slowing down the rate of reactions catalysed by enzymes and reducing the growth rate of spoilage-causing bacteria, which are both more active at higher temperatures.

How Do Batteries Store Energy?

Batteries store energy in a chemical form and convert it into electrical energy. To understand how they work, it's important to know about electrons and electrical currents.

Electrons are tiny particles with a negative charge, found in all atoms. When electrons move through a conductor, like a metal wire, they create an electrical current. This current is what powers electronic devices.

A basic battery has three main components: two electrodes (an anode and a cathode) and an electrolyte. The anode is the negative end, and the cathode is the positive end. The electrolyte is a substance that allows electric charge to move between the anode and cathode.

In a battery, a chemical reaction occurs at the anode, releasing electrons. These electrons flow through an external circuit (the device you're powering) to the cathode, creating an electrical current. Meanwhile, ions in the electrolyte move between the electrodes to balance the charge.

You can demonstrate a simple version of this with a lemon battery at home. A lemon battery includes a lemon (as the electrolyte) and two different metals, like a copper penny (cathode) and a zinc nail (anode). The lemon's juice, rich in citric acid, acts as the electrolyte.

When you insert the two metals into the lemon, the zinc starts to react with the acid. This reaction releases electrons at the zinc anode, which then flow to the copper cathode, creating an electric current. This current can be harnessed to power a small device, like an LED light.

This homemade battery illustrates the basic principles of how batteries work. The chemical reaction between the zinc and the citric acid creates a flow of electrons (electrical current), demonstrating how chemical energy is transformed into electrical energy. It's a simple yet effective way to understand the fundamentals of battery science.

Why Do Chargers get Hot if you Leave them Plugged in too Long?

Chargers getting hot when left plugged in for extended periods is related to electrical resistance and the nature of how chargers work. Understanding this requires a basic knowledge of how electricity flows and what happens when it encounters resistance.

Electricity flows through the charger to power a device or charge its battery. This flow involves electrons moving through the charger's components. As they move, they encounter resistance. Resistance is a natural property of all materials to some degree; it's the opposition to the flow of electric current.

When electrons encounter resistance, they don't stop, but their interaction with the material's atoms causes energy to be released. This energy is released in the form of heat. The more resistance there is, the more heat is produced. This is due to the principle known as Joule heating (or resistive heating), where the energy lost due to resistance is converted into heat.

Chargers, especially those converting AC (alternating current from your home power supply) to DC (direct current, used by most of your devices), have components like transformers and rectifiers which experience resistance and, hence, heat up during operation. When left plugged in, even without actively charging a device, these components still encounter electrical resistance and continue to produce heat.

Moreover, inefficiencies in the charger's design can exacerbate this heating. Older or lower-quality chargers often have higher resistance and less efficient conversion processes, leading to more heat generation.

It's important to note that while chargers are designed to handle some heat, excessive heating can be a safety hazard and reduce the charger's lifespan. This is why it's generally recommended to unplug chargers when not in use, both to save energy and to minimize the risk of overheating and potential damage.

In summary, chargers heat up due to electrical resistance, which converts some of the electrical energy into heat. This is a normal part of how chargers work, but leaving them plugged in for too long can lead to unnecessary heat buildup and potential safety risks.

How Do Wireless Chargers Work?

Wireless chargers work using a technology known as electromagnetic induction, which involves electromagnetic fields and waves. To understand this, it's helpful to first know a bit about electromagnetic (EM) waves.

EM waves are a form of energy that can travel through space. They include a variety of types, like radio waves, microwaves, infrared, visible light, ultraviolet, X-rays, and gamma rays. These waves are used in many technologies, from radios and cell phones to medical equipment.

In the context of wireless charging, the key part is the use of a specific range of EM waves - typically radio waves or microwaves. Wireless charging systems consist of two main components: a transmitter (the charging pad) and a receiver (built into the device being charged). Both parts have coils: the transmitter has a coil that generates an electromagnetic field, and the receiver has a coil that captures energy from this field.

Here's how it works:

1. **Power Conversion**: The charging pad is plugged into a power source, converting

electrical power from the outlet into an electromagnetic field.

2. **Generating EM Waves:** This conversion happens through a process known as induction. When electric current flows through the coil in the charging pad, it creates an electromagnetic field around it.

3. **Inducing Current in the Receiver:** The electromagnetic field then induces a current in the coil of the receiving device. This is possible because when a coil is exposed to a changing electromagnetic field, an electric current is generated within it - a principle known as electromagnetic induction.

4. **Power to the Device:** The induced current in the receiver coil is then converted back into electric power, which charges the battery of the device.

Wireless charging technology is a practical application of electromagnetic principles. It uses EM waves to transfer energy from a charging pad to a device without the need for wires. This technology not only offers the convenience of charging without cables but also demonstrates the versatility and importance of electromagnetic waves in modern technology.

Why Does Nothing Stick to Teflon?

The reason why nothing sticks to Teflon, a brand name for a polymer known as polytetrafluoroethylene (PTFE), lies in its unique molecular structure. This structure gives Teflon its non-stick properties, which have made it popular in cookware and various industrial applications.

PTFE is a long chain polymer, composed of carbon and fluorine atoms. The key to its non-stick nature is the fluorine atoms, which are extremely electronegative. This means they strongly attract electrons, creating a surface that is both slippery and chemically unreactive.

In PTFE, each carbon atom is bonded to two fluorine atoms. The fluorine atoms create a protective shield around the carbon atoms, preventing other substances from sticking to or reacting with them. This shield is so effective that not only do food particles not adhere to it, but also most adhesives and substances fail to make a lasting bond with the material.

The non-reactive nature of PTFE also means that it's resistant to a wide range of chemicals, making it useful in many industrial applications where corrosion resistance is essential. Additionally, PTFE has a high melting point and low friction coefficient, further enhancing its usefulness in various settings.

It's worth noting that while Teflon's non-stick property is a significant advantage, it should be used carefully in cookware. At very high temperatures (above 260°C or 500°F), PTFE can start to decompose, releasing fumes that can be harmful if inhaled.

In summary, Teflon's non-stick property is due to the molecular structure of PTFE, particularly the presence of fluorine atoms that create a slippery and chemically inert surface. This unique characteristic makes it an invaluable material in both the kitchen and industrial applications.

Why are Rocks so Hard?

Rocks, the building blocks of the Earth's crust, owe their hardness to the molecular structure and bonding within the minerals they are composed of. Many rocks are incredibly hard because they contain minerals with large covalent structures, where atoms are bonded together by shared electrons.

In covalent bonding, atoms share pairs of electrons, creating a strong bond that is difficult to break. This type of bonding is prevalent in many minerals that form rocks. When these covalent bonds extend over a large network of atoms, they create large covalent structures that are extremely strong and hard.

For example, quartz, a common mineral found in many types of rock, has a crystalline structure where each silicon atom is bonded to four oxygen atoms in a tetrahedral shape. These tetrahedra are then linked together in a continuous network, with each oxygen atom shared between two silicon atoms. This extensive network of strong covalent bonds gives quartz its great hardness.

Diamond, another example, though not a common component of rocks, perfectly illustrates the concept of a large covalent structure. In diamonds, each carbon atom is bonded to four other carbon atoms in a strong, tetrahedral lattice. This continuous network of covalent bonds throughout the crystal makes diamond one of the hardest substances known.

The strength and arrangement of these covalent bonds determine the hardness of the mineral and, consequently, the rock. Rocks composed of minerals with strong, extensive covalent bonding tend to be harder. However, not all rocks are equally hard. The overall hardness of a rock also depends on other factors, including the size and interlocking nature of the mineral grains and the presence of any weaker bonds or structures within the rock.

In essence, the hardness of rocks is a direct consequence of the microscopic structures and bonds within the minerals they contain, with large covalent structures playing a key role in making certain rocks particularly hard and resistant to wear.

Why is Ice Slippy?

The slipperiness of ice is a phenomenon that's intrigued scientists for years. It's not just the ice itself that's slippery, but rather the very thin layer of water that forms on its surface. This slipperiness can be attributed to several factors, including the effects of pressure and temperature on the melting point of ice.

Firstly, when pressure is applied to ice, such as when someone steps on it, it can cause the ice to melt locally. This is due to the fact that increasing pressure lowers the melting point of ice. Under normal atmospheric conditions, ice melts at 0°C (32°F). However, when pressure is applied, it requires a lower temperature for the ice to remain solid. This phenomenon is described by the phase diagram of water, where the melting point of ice decreases with increasing pressure. So, when you stand or skate on ice, the pressure of your weight can momentarily melt the top layer, creating a thin film of water. This water layer is much slipperier than solid ice, leading to the slippery surface.

Additionally, the surface of ice naturally possesses a thin layer of liquid-like water molecules, even without any added pressure. This is because the molecules at the surface of the ice are not as tightly packed as those within the ice, allowing them to move more freely. This quasi-liquid layer reduces friction and contributes to the slipperiness.

Temperature also influences this process. As the temperature of ice approaches its melting point, the number of molecules in the surface liquid-like layer increases, enhancing slipperiness. Conversely, extremely cold ice has a less pronounced liquid layer and may not be as slippery.

In summary, the slipperiness of ice is a complex interplay of factors. Pressure lowers the melting point of ice, leading to the formation of a thin layer of water. The presence of a quasi-liquid layer on the surface of the ice, along with temperature effects, further contributes to reducing friction. Understanding these aspects provides insight into the intriguing physical properties of ice and water.

Why does ice float on water?

Ice floating on water is a remarkable phenomenon, and it's essential for life as we know it. This behaviour is unusual because, in most substances, the solid form is denser than the liquid form and sinks. However, water and ice behave differently due to the molecular structure of water.

Water is composed of two hydrogen atoms and one oxygen atom (H_2O). The unique property of ice floating on water is due to the way water molecules arrange themselves when they freeze. In liquid water, the molecules are close together but move freely. As water cools and starts to freeze, these molecules arrange themselves into a crystalline structure. This structure is a hexagonal lattice that creates more open space than in the liquid state.

The open crystalline structure in ice results in lower density compared to liquid water. Density is a measure of mass per unit volume, and because the same number of water molecules occupies more space when solidified into ice, ice is less dense than water. Hence, ice floats on water.

The fact that ice floats is crucial for life on Earth, especially in aquatic ecosystems. If ice sank, bodies of water would freeze from the bottom up, drastically altering the environment for aquatic life. Since ice floats, it forms a protective surface layer that insulates the water below, maintaining a stable and liveable environment even in cold climates. This insulation is crucial for survival of aquatic organisms through winter, as the liquid water beneath the ice stays at a life-sustaining temperature.

In summary, ice floats on water because of its unique molecular structure, which makes it less dense in its solid form. This unusual property is vital for sustaining aquatic ecosystems and plays a significant role in Earth's climate system, underlining the unique characteristics of water that are essential for life.

How Does Pressure Cooking Make Food Cook Faster?

Pressure cooking is an efficient method of cooking food quickly, and its effectiveness can be explained by understanding the concepts of boiling, and how liquids and gases behave under pressure.

Boiling is the process where a liquid turns into a gas. This occurs when the liquid's temperature reaches its boiling point, the temperature at which the pressure of the vapor (gas) escaping from the liquid equals the surrounding pressure. At sea level, water boils at 100°C (212°F). However, the boiling point can change with pressure, which is where the pressure cooker comes into play.

A pressure cooker is a sealed pot with a valve that controls the steam pressure inside. As the pot heats up, the liquid inside forms steam, increasing the pressure in the sealed environment. This higher pressure has two main effects:

Increased Boiling Point: Under higher pressure, the boiling point of water (or any liquid) increases. In a pressure cooker, this can reach as high as 120°C (248°F). Since the water (or cooking liquid) can get hotter before it boils, it cooks the food at a higher temperature than possible with conventional boiling in an open pot.

Forced Steam Penetration: The high pressure also forces steam and moisture into the food, which can help it cook faster. This is particularly effective for tough cuts of meat or hard legumes and grains, which benefit from both the higher temperature and the forced moisture.

Cooking under high pressure can significantly reduce cooking times - often to one-third of the time needed for traditional cooking methods. Additionally, because less water is needed compared to boiling or simmering, nutrients are less likely to be dissolved away, making pressure cooking a healthier cooking option.

In summary, pressure cooking accelerates the cooking process by increasing the boiling point of water within a sealed environment, allowing food to be cooked at higher temperatures, and the high pressure also helps in better penetration of moisture into the food. This method showcases an interesting application of the physical properties of liquids and gases under varying pressure.

What Causes Rust to Form on Metal Objects?

Rust formation on metal objects, particularly iron and steel, is a common example of a chemical reaction between a metal and oxygen, known as oxidation. This process is part of a broader category of reactions where metals react with oxygen, often leading to corrosion.

Rust specifically refers to iron oxide, which forms when iron reacts with oxygen and water. This process is accelerated in the presence of saltwater or acidic conditions. The basic chemical reaction for the formation of rust can be simplified as follows: iron (Fe) reacts with oxygen (O_2) in the air and water (H_2O) to form iron oxide (Fe_2O_3), commonly known as rust.

The process begins with the iron surface coming into contact with water and oxygen. Water, especially when it contains dissolved salts or carbon dioxide, acts as an electrolyte, facilitating the movement of electrons. When iron atoms lose electrons (a process known as oxidation), they form iron ions (Fe^{2+}). At the same time, oxygen in the air gains these electrons (a process known as reduction) and forms hydroxide ions (OH^-). These ions react with the iron ions to form iron oxide, which appears as the reddish-brown crust we know as rust.

This oxidation process is not unique to iron; other metals also undergo similar reactions. For instance, when copper oxidizes, it forms a greenish layer called patina, and aluminium forms a white, powdery aluminium oxide layer. However, unlike rust, which can flake off and expose more metal to corrosion, the oxidation layers on metals like aluminium and copper can actually protect the underlying metal from further corrosion.

Rust is problematic because it not only affects the appearance of metal objects but also compromises their structural integrity. Iron oxide is more brittle and less dense than iron, so rusted metal is weaker and more prone to breaking.

In summary, rust forms on metal objects due to the chemical reaction between iron, oxygen, and water. This process, a type of oxidation, is a common problem that illustrates the reactive nature of metals when exposed to certain environmental conditions. The study of these reactions is important in fields like materials science and conservation, where understanding and preventing corrosion is crucial.

Why Doesn't Gold Rust or Tarnish like Other Metals?

You have probably seen pictures of ancient gold objects recovered from archaeological digs that look almost brand new. This remarkable preservation is due to gold's chemical properties, especially its low reactivity compared to other metals. Understanding why gold doesn't rust or tarnish like other metals involves exploring the concepts of reactivity and the reactivity series in chemistry.

Reactivity refers to how easily a substance participates in chemical reactions. In the context of metals, this is often gauged by how readily a metal reacts with substances like oxygen and water, which can lead to corrosion such as rusting or tarnishing.

The reactivity series is a ranking of metals based on their reactivity. Metals at the top, like lithium and potassium, are highly reactive, especially with water and oxygen. Iron, which is lower in the series, is less reactive but still prone to rusting, forming iron oxide.

Gold, however, is positioned near the bottom of this reactivity series, indicating its low reactivity. Its resistance to reacting with oxygen and water means that it does not rust or tarnish. This inertness is why gold maintains its shiny, lustrous appearance over time, making it ideal for jewellery and ornamental objects.

Unlike gold, other metals like silver and copper, while less reactive than iron, can still tarnish over time. Silver, for instance, reacts with sulphur-containing substances in the air, leading to tarnishing.

Gold's enduring shine and lack of corrosion, as evidenced by ancient artifacts, are a testament to its chemical stability. Its position in the reactivity series explains why it has been treasured through the ages, not just for its beauty but also for its ability to withstand the test of time without deteriorating.

Why is Gold Shiny?

Gold's characteristic shine is a result of its metallic properties, particularly its ability to reflect light. Metals, in general, have a lustrous appearance because of how their electrons behave.

In metals, some of the electrons are not bound to any particular atom. Instead, they move freely throughout the metal's crystal lattice. This free movement of electrons is what gives metals their conductivity. When light, which is an electromagnetic wave, hits the surface of a metal like gold, these free electrons absorb and then re-emit the light. This process of absorption and re-emission results in the reflection of light, giving metals their shiny appearance.

Gold, in particular, is highly reflective and does not corrode or tarnish in air or water, which means its shiny surface is not dulled by oxidation over time. The unique electronic structure of gold also contributes to its rich, yellow colour. While most metals reflect all wavelengths of light, giving them a silvery appearance, gold's electron configuration leads it to absorb some wavelengths of blue light. This absorption results in the reflection of a yellowish light, combining with its metallic lustre to produce the distinctive golden shine.

In summary, gold is shiny because of its metallic nature, where the free movement of electrons on its surface leads to efficient reflection of light. Its resistance to tarnishing and unique electronic structure give it both its lustre and characteristic gold colour.

Why is Diamond so Hard?

Diamond's renowned hardness, the highest of any natural material, is largely attributed to its giant covalent structure. Understanding this aspect of its atomic arrangement sheds light on why diamonds are so uniquely hard.

In a diamond, each carbon atom is covalently bonded to four other carbon atoms in a tetrahedral structure. This means every carbon atom shares electrons with its neighbours in a very strong type of chemical bond known as a covalent bond. The covalent bonds in diamonds are particularly robust due to the equal sharing of electrons between carbon atoms.

The arrangement of carbon atoms in a diamond forms a giant covalent structure, meaning it extends throughout the entire structure of the diamond. This continuous network of strongly bonded atoms provides an incredible level of strength and durability. In a diamond, these bonds form a rigid, three-dimensional lattice that resists deformation. When force is applied to a diamond, it's spread out over many strong bonds, making it extremely hard for the structure to break apart.

This giant covalent structure is what sets diamond apart from other forms of carbon, like graphite. In graphite, carbon atoms are also bonded covalently, but in layers that are only weakly held together. This difference in atomic bonding is why graphite is soft and slippery, while diamond is extraordinarily hard.

Diamond's hardness has practical applications in cutting, drilling, and polishing, as few materials can scratch or cut through its structure. At the same time, this property makes diamonds highly valued as gemstones for their enduring beauty and resistance to scratching.

In summary, diamond's exceptional hardness is a result of its giant covalent structure, where each carbon atom is strongly bonded to four others in a three-dimensional lattice. This arrangement gives diamonds their unmatched strength and resistance to being scratched or broken.

How do fireworks get their colours?

The vibrant colours in fireworks come from the use of various metal salts and compounds that emit specific colours when burned. These colours are a result of the heat of the explosion exciting the electrons in the metal atoms, causing them to emit light.

Each metal or metal compound produces a characteristic colour. For instance, sodium compounds emit a yellow colour, barium yields green, calcium creates an orange hue, copper burns blue, and strontium produces red. The specific colour is determined by the wavelengths of light emitted by the excited electrons of these metals. When the electrons return to their original energy state, they release energy in the form of light. The colour of this light depends on the energy difference between the excited state and the ground state of the electrons.

To create different colours, pyrotechnicians mix these metal salts with the explosive compounds in the fireworks. When the firework explodes, the heat from the explosion excites the electrons in the metal atoms, and as they return to their ground state, they emit light in the characteristic colours.

How do Desalination Plants Turn Seawater into Drinking Water?

Desalination plants turn seawater into drinking water through a process that removes salt and other minerals. This is important because seawater is too salty to drink and can be harmful to the human body. The two most common methods used in desalination are distillation and reverse osmosis.

In distillation, seawater is heated until it turns into steam. This steam is basically water in the form of gas, and it leaves the salt behind. Then, the steam is cooled down and turns back into liquid water. This water is now fresh and can be drunk. It's like boiling water to make steam and then cooling the steam to make water again, but without the salt.

Reverse osmosis is a bit different. In this method, seawater is pushed through a special filter. This filter, or membrane, has very tiny holes. The holes are so small that they only let water molecules pass through and leave the larger salt molecules behind. It's like using a very fine sieve that only lets the tiny bits go through.

Both these methods need a lot of energy. Distillation needs heat to boil the water, and reverse osmosis needs pressure to push the water through the filter. That's why desalination can be expensive.

Once the water is desalinated, it might be treated further to make it suitable for drinking. This includes adding minerals or other treatments to make sure it's safe and tastes good.

In summary, desalination plants make drinking water from seawater by removing salt. They mainly do this by either heating the water to make steam and then cooling it, or by pushing the water through a filter that catches the salt. This process is crucial for providing fresh water in places where it's scarce.

Why Can't I Drink Salty Water?

Drinking salty water is harmful due to the principles of osmosis and the body's inability to process excessive amounts of salt effectively.

Osmosis is the movement of water through a semipermeable membrane (like cell membranes in our bodies) from an area of lower solute concentration to an area of higher solute concentration. It aims to equalize the solute concentrations on both sides of the membrane.

When you drink salty water, the high concentration of salt in the water leads to an imbalance between the salt concentration in your bloodstream and that within your body's cells. Normally, the body maintains a delicate balance of salt and water concentrations. However, introducing a large amount of salt disrupts this balance.

In response to the higher concentration of salt in the bloodstream, water molecules move out of the body cells and into the bloodstream to dilute the excess salt. This movement of water out of the cells leads to cellular dehydration. The dehydrated cells signal the brain, which interprets this as thirst, prompting you to drink more water.

Moreover, the human kidneys have a limit in filtering excess salt from the bloodstream. When this limit is exceeded, as it would be by drinking seawater, the kidneys cannot remove all the excess salt without losing a significant amount of water. This results in a net loss of water, further dehydrating the body.

In summary, drinking salty water is harmful because it leads to cellular dehydration through osmosis and exceeds the kidneys' ability to filter and excrete excess salt. This imbalance causes the body to lose more water than it gains, leading to increased thirst and potential dehydration, rather than alleviating it.

Why is the Sea Salty?

The sea is salty primarily due to the process of erosion and the way rivers transport minerals and salts from the land to the ocean. This natural process has been occurring for millions of years, contributing to the salinity of our oceans.

Erosion is the process by which soil and rock are removed from the Earth's surface by natural forces such as wind and water flow, and then transported and deposited in other locations. When rain falls, it interacts with carbon dioxide in the atmosphere and the Earth's surface, forming a weak carbonic acid. As this slightly acidic rainwater flows over the land, it erodes the rocks. This process causes the minerals and salts contained in the rocks to be released into the water.

These dissolved minerals, including salts primarily composed of sodium and chloride, are then carried by rivers and streams to the oceans. Over millions of years, these rivers have continually flowed into the ocean, depositing salts. While water evaporates from the ocean's surface, the salts do not. This means that over time, the concentration of salt in the ocean has gradually increased, leading to its current salinity.

Additionally, underwater volcanic activity and hydrothermal vents also contribute to the ocean's salinity by releasing minerals and salts from beneath the Earth's crust.

While the concentration of salt in the ocean remains relatively stable now, it is the result of this long-term accumulation process, driven significantly by erosion and the continuous cycle of rainwater dissolving minerals and carrying them to the sea.

In summary, the sea is salty due to the process of erosion, where rainwater dissolves minerals and salts from rocks and soil, which are then carried by rivers into the oceans. This natural process, combined with contributions from underwater geological activity, has led to the accumulation of salts in the ocean over millions of years.

What Causes Earthquakes?

Earthquakes are primarily caused by the movement of the Earth's tectonic plates, a process explained by the theory of plate tectonics. This theory provides an understanding of the Earth's surface as a dynamic system made up of large plates of crust that float on the semi-fluid asthenosphere beneath.

The Earth's crust is divided into several major and minor plates. These tectonic plates are constantly moving, albeit very slowly, typically at a rate of a few centimetres per year. This movement is driven by the heat from the Earth's interior, which causes convection currents in the mantle.

Earthquakes occur mainly at the boundaries of these tectonic plates. There are three types of plate boundaries: convergent (where plates move towards each other), divergent (where plates move apart), and transform (where plates slide past each other). Earthquakes at these boundaries are caused by different mechanisms:

Convergent Boundaries: At these boundaries, one plate may be forced beneath another in a process known as subduction. The immense pressure and friction can cause the edge of the plate to become stuck. When the stress on the plate overcomes the friction, it releases suddenly, causing an earthquake.

Divergent Boundaries: Here, plates move apart, and new crust is formed from magma rising to the surface. As the plates separate, the release of tension and settling of new crust can result in earthquakes.

Transform Boundaries: Earthquakes at these boundaries occur as plates slide past each other. The friction between the plates prevents smooth movement, and when the stress builds up and is suddenly released, it causes an earthquake.

Most earthquakes are relatively minor and may not be felt, but larger ones can be destructive. The point on the Earth's surface directly above the earthquake's origin (the focus) is called the epicentre.

In summary, earthquakes are caused by the movement of the Earth's tectonic plates, particularly at their boundaries. The release of energy due to the movement, collision, or sliding of these plates against each other is what we experience as earthquakes.

How Do Earthquakes Cause Tsunamis?

Earthquakes can cause tsunamis, particularly when they occur under the ocean. These underwater earthquakes typically happen along tectonic plate boundaries *(see previous question),* where massive slabs of the Earth's crust are either colliding, sliding past each other, or moving apart.

When these plates shift abruptly during an earthquake, the sea floor can be uplifted or displaced, displacing a huge volume of water above it. This displacement creates powerful waves that start to travel across the ocean surface. Unlike normal ocean waves, which are caused by wind and only affect the surface layer, tsunami waves involve the movement of the entire water column, from the ocean surface to the sea floor.

As these waves travel towards the shore, they gain height. The reason for this is that the ocean becomes shallower near the coast, which causes the tsunami waves to slow down in speed but increase in height. By the time these waves reach the shore, they can be very tall and powerful, capable of causing significant destruction.

Why are there Mountains?

Mountains are majestic natural formations that arise due to the movements and interactions of the Earth's tectonic plates, as explained by the theory of plate tectonics. These plates are massive sections of the Earth's crust floating over a semi-fluid layer beneath, and their activities over millions of years lead to the formation of mountains.

One common way mountains form is at convergent plate boundaries where two tectonic plates move towards each other. When continental plates collide, they can't easily subduct or go beneath each other due to their buoyancy. Instead, they crumple and fold, pushing the crust upwards to form mountain ranges, such as the Himalayas, created by the collision of the Indian and Eurasian plates.

In subduction zones, where an oceanic plate dives beneath a continental plate, the edge of the continental plate is crumpled and uplifted, forming mountains. The process can also trigger volcanic activity as the subducting plate melts, contributing to the formation of mountains like those in the Andes range.

Volcanic activity is another way mountains are formed. During eruptions, volcanoes spew out lava, ash, and other materials that accumulate around the vent. Over time, this material builds up to form volcanic mountains, like Mount Fuji in Japan.

Faulting, where cracks in the Earth's crust cause large blocks of crust to move up or down, also leads to mountain formation. The uplifted blocks from such movements can form impressive mountain ranges.

Through these various processes, mountains are not just formed but also continue to evolve, highlighting the dynamic nature of the Earth's crust. They serve as a testament to the immense geological forces at work beneath our feet and play a crucial role in shaping the planet's landscape.

Why are the Himalayas higher than the Alps?

The Himalayas are higher than the Alps primarily due to the nature of the tectonic plate interactions that formed them and the relative age of these mountain ranges.

The Himalayas were formed by the collision between the Indian Plate and the Eurasian Plate. This collision, which began about 50 million years ago and continues today, is a major tectonic event. The Indian Plate is moving northward at a rate of about 5 cm per year and is being forced under the Eurasian Plate. This ongoing process has created the highest mountain range in the world, with several peaks, including Mount Everest, rising over 8,000 meters above sea level.

In contrast, the Alps were formed by the collision of the African Plate and the Eurasian Plate, but this collision is less intense than that of the Himalayas. The Alps are also much older than the Himalayas, having started to form around 65 million years ago. Over time, erosion and other geological processes have worn down the Alps, whereas the Himalayas, being younger, are still rising and subject to less erosion comparatively.

Another factor contributing to the height of the Himalayas is the type of crust involved in their formation. The Indian and Eurasian plates are both continental crusts, which are thick and buoyant. When they collide, the crust is pushed up more dramatically, leading to the formation of very high mountains. In the case of the Alps, the collision involves thinner oceanic crust from the African Plate and the thicker continental crust of the Eurasian Plate, leading to a less dramatic uplift.

What Are Stars?

Stars, the sparkling dots we see in the night sky, are actually massive, luminous spheres of plasma held together by their own gravity. They are fundamental to the cosmos, playing a key role in the structure and evolution of galaxies, including our own Milky Way.

At the heart of a star is a process called nuclear fusion. This process takes place in the star's core and involves the fusion of hydrogen atoms into helium under extremely high temperatures and pressures. This fusion releases a tremendous amount of energy, which radiates outward into space as both light and heat, making the star shine.

The life cycle of a star is determined by its mass. Larger stars, which have more mass, burn their fuel more quickly and have shorter lifespans. Smaller stars, like our Sun, consume their fuel more slowly and can shine for billions of years. Over its lifetime, a star undergoes various stages, starting as a nebula, a cloud of gas and dust, then evolving into a main-sequence star, and finally into its end stages, which can be a white dwarf, neutron star, or black hole, depending on the initial mass of the star.

The colour of a star is indicative of its surface temperature. Hotter stars appear blue or white, while cooler stars appear red or orange. This colour variation is due to differences in the wavelengths of light emitted at different temperatures.

Stars are not only important as individual celestial objects, but they also play a crucial role in the universe. They are the factories where most of the elements heavier than hydrogen and helium are formed. These elements are essential for the formation of planets and life as we know it. When stars end their lives, especially in explosive events like supernovae, they scatter these elements into space, where they can eventually become part of new stars, planets, and even living organisms.

In summary, stars are massive, glowing spheres of plasma, powered by nuclear fusion in their cores. They vary in size, colour, and lifespan, and their existence and evolution are central to the workings of the universe, contributing to the creation of the elements that make up the world around us.

How Do Stars Form?

Stars begin their life in giant clouds of dust and gas called nebulae. Here's how these twinkling objects in the night sky are born:

Nebula Shrinks: A nebula starts to shrink or collapse, often triggered by something like a nearby star exploding. As it collapses, it gets denser and hotter in the centre.

Protostar Forms: In the middle of this shrinking cloud, a protostar forms. This is like a baby star. It's not hot enough yet for nuclear fusion, the process that makes stars really shine.

Nuclear Fusion Starts: As the protostar gathers more gas and dust, it gets hotter and denser. When it's hot enough, nuclear fusion begins. This is where hydrogen atoms join to make helium and release a lot of energy – this makes the star shine.

Becoming a Star: Once nuclear fusion is stable, the star enters what's called the main sequence phase. This is the adult stage of a star's life, where it shines steadily for millions to billions of years. Our Sun is in this stage right now.

Why is Mars Red?

Mars, often called the "Red Planet," owes its distinctive colour to a mineral called iron oxide, commonly known as rust, which covers its surface.

The Martian soil and rocks have a lot of iron in them. This iron reacts with the small amounts of oxygen present in the thin Martian atmosphere, creating iron oxide. Iron oxide has a reddish-brown colour, which gives Mars its reddish appearance, both from space and from the surface.

This process is similar to the rusting that happens on Earth when iron is exposed to oxygen and water. However, on Mars, the process is much slower and drier. The planet's atmosphere has only trace amounts of oxygen and water vapor, so the iron oxide forms over millions of years as these elements slowly react with the surface minerals.

In summary, Mars is red due to the presence of iron oxide, or rust, on its surface, which forms over a long period due to the reaction of iron in Martian rocks and soil with oxygen in the thin atmosphere.

Why do Planets Orbit the Sun and not Fall into the Sun?

Planets orbit the sun and don't fall into it due to a balance between two key forces: gravity and their orbital velocity.

Gravity is the force that attracts objects with mass towards each other. In the case of the solar system, the sun, being much more massive than the planets, exerts a strong gravitational pull on them. This gravitational force is what initially pulls the planets towards the sun.

However, planets don't just fall into the sun because they are also moving sideways at a significant speed. This motion is known as orbital velocity. When a planet moves sideways at the right speed, the curve of its path matches the curve of the space it is being pulled into by gravity. This creates an orbit.

This balance can be thought of as a continuous fall towards the sun, but the forward motion of the planet causes it to keep missing the sun. This is similar to how a satellite orbits Earth: it's falling towards Earth due to gravity, but its forward motion keeps it in orbit.

In essence, the orbit of a planet is a constant balance between the pull of the sun's gravity and the planet's sideways motion. If the forward motion were too slow, the planet would spiral into the sun. If it were too fast, it would escape the sun's gravitational pull and move out into space. The stable orbits of the planets are a result of billions of years of gravitational interaction in the solar system.

Why Does the Earth Rotate?

Earth's rotation, the spinning motion on its axis, is a result of how our planet was formed over 4.5 billion years ago. When the solar system was forming, it began as a giant, rotating cloud of gas and dust. As this cloud collapsed under its own gravity, it started to spin faster due to the conservation of angular momentum, a principle in physics that describes how an object's rotational speed will increase as it shrinks in size, much like a figure skater pulling in their arms to spin faster.

Most of the material in this cloud eventually formed the sun, but the leftover bits and pieces coalesced to form the planets, including Earth. As these materials clumped together to form Earth, they retained some of this rotational motion.

This initial spinning motion has been maintained over billions of years due to the lack of significant external forces in space to slow it down. In space, without much friction to oppose its motion, Earth continues to rotate on its axis, leading to the cycle of day and night that we experience.

Is it True that Atoms Never Touch?

You may have heard someone use the excuse 'I didn't hit them because atoms never touch' from one of your classmates." This statement, while amusing, actually touches on a fundamental concept in physics about the nature of atomic interactions.

Atoms, the basic building blocks of matter, are composed of a nucleus surrounded by electrons. These electrons are in constant motion around the nucleus and create a sort of 'electron cloud'. The electron cloud generates a force field around the atom, which is essentially a region of electrical charge.

When two atoms come close to each other, the electron clouds experience a force. If the atoms get too close, the electron clouds start to repel each other due to the Pauli exclusion principle, which states that no two electrons can occupy the same quantum state simultaneously. This repulsion is what gives matter its solidness. So, when you touch something, you are feeling the force of the electrons in your atoms repelling the electrons in the atoms of the object you are touching.

In essence, the sensation of touch is actually the electromagnetic force of repulsion between electrons. The nuclei of the atoms in your hand never actually 'touch' the nuclei of the atoms in the object. This atomic interaction is why you feel resistance when you push against a solid object, even though, on an atomic level, the particles are not physically making contact in the traditional sense.

So, while the statement from your classmate may sound like a clever excuse, it is rooted in the reality of how atomic interactions work. The sensation of touch is the result of electromagnetic forces, not the direct contact of atoms.

Epilogue

There are infinitely more questions you could ask about the world than those posed in this short book. Almost any object you look, or anything you do through the day could lead to another question. I hope you start thinking up some of these questions, and then go looking for the answer.

Printed in Great Britain
by Amazon

34514231R00059